Communicate!
Pop Song Lyrics

Dona Herweck Rice

Publishing Credits

Rachelle Cracchiolo, M.S.Ed., *Publisher*
Conni Medina, M.A.Ed., *Managing Editor*
Nika Fabienke, Ed.D., *Series Developer*
June Kikuchi, *Content Director*
John Leach, *Assistant Editor*
Lee Aucoin, *Senior Graphic Designer*

TIME For Kids and the TIME For Kids logo are registered trademarks of TIME Inc. Used under license.

Image Credits: p.24 GraficallyMinded/Alamy Stock Photo; all other images from iStock and/or Shutterstock

All companies and products mentioned in this book are registered trademarks of their respective owners or developers and are used in this book strictly for editorial purposes; no commercial claim to their use is made by the author or the publisher.

Library of Congress Cataloging-in-Publication Data
Names: Rice, Dona.
Title: Communicate! Pop song lyrics / Dona Herweck Rice.
Description: Huntington Beach, CA : Teacher Created Materials, [2017] | Includes index.
Identifiers: LCCN 2017013463 (print) | LCCN 2017013968 (ebook) | ISBN 9781425853471 (eBook) | ISBN 9781425849733 (pbk.)
Subjects: LCSH: Popular music--History and criticism--Juvenile literature. | Popular music--Writing and publishing--Juvenile literature.
Classification: LCC ML3928 (ebook) | LCC ML3928 .R5 2017 (print) | DDC 782.42164--dc23
LC record available at https://lccn.loc.gov/2017013463

Teacher Created Materials
5301 Oceanus Drive
Huntington Beach, CA 92649-1030
http://www.tcmpub.com
ISBN 978-1-4258-4973-3
© 2018 Teacher Created Materials, Inc.

Table of Contents

Pop!	4
Shoo-bop Shoo-bop	6
What Makes a Great Lyric?	14
Words Matter	22
That Would Make a Great Song!	26
Glossary	28
Index	29
Check It Out!	30
Try It!	31
About the Author	32

Pop!

Pop up. Popcorn. Pop fly. Pop music?

To pop is to make a little explosion. POP! And maybe pop music does explode a bit. It explodes in people's minds and makes them want to sing. It explodes in people's feet and makes them want to dance. It explodes through communities and becomes something everyone talks about and enjoys.

The "pop" in pop music is short for "popular." Pop is popular music. Every year there are new pop hits. Back in 1922, "Yes! We Have No Bananas" thrilled listeners. "Chattanooga Choo Choo" stirred them up in 1941. "Kung Fu Fighting" was a 1974 sensation. A more recent pop hit is "Uptown Funk."

Number One

The Beatles were a popular band with many number-one songs. John Lennon and Paul McCartney were two members of the band. Lennon wrote 22 number one songs. McCartney wrote 36.

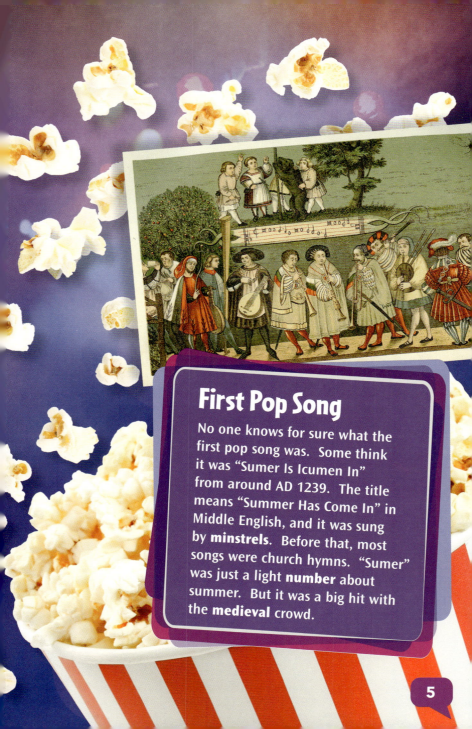

First Pop Song

No one knows for sure what the first pop song was. Some think it was "Sumer Is Icumen In" from around AD 1239. The title means "Summer Has Come In" in Middle English, and it was sung by **minstrels**. Before that, most songs were church hymns. "Sumer" was just a light **number** about summer. But it was a big hit with the **medieval** crowd.

Shoo-bop Shoo-bop

"What are they talking about?!"

Parents have been trying to figure out pop music since pop music began. A cave child probably once sang, "Shoo-bop, shoo-bop." Then, her cave dad cried out, "I just don't get you kids!"

Pop is a **genre** that many people think is for young people. That could be because people tend to best like the songs from when they were young. Older people often think that new songs are not as good as the ones they heard as kids. This is just human nature.

Each **generation** has its own pop music. Kids love their new music for the same reasons their parents loved theirs.

That's Cool, Daddy-o!

There are a lot of **slang** words that mean "good." Surprisingly, some slang we use now is over 100 years old. Your great-grandparents probably said "cool" for "good," just as you say it today. What new slang might your grandkids say?

What's to Love?

Why do people love pop music so much? Maybe it is the music itself. You can easily sing or dance along to a great pop song, and maybe the beat or groove makes you feel a certain way. You may feel happy or sad, and either emotion can be satisfying. You may feel hopeful, inspired, or fired up! A good song can make you feel any of these and more.

Of course, the music in a song is important. It would not be a song without it. What about the lyrics? How important are they, and what makes one lyric better than another? Would "Yes! We Have No Broccoli" be just as good a lyric as "No Bananas"? People might not like it as much.

"Yes! We have no bananas. We have no bananas today!"

Music and Speech

Scientists have found that the patterns in happy songs reflect our patterns of happy speech. The same is true for sad music and sad speech. In some ways, songs mirror the ways we talk.

Lyrics Matter

Words are one of the most important parts of our lives. They are a major way we connect with each other. We speak, write, read, text, watch television, and listen to music almost constantly. Without words, we would lose a major source of connection. We might even find it hard to live without them.

Words are a pretty big deal, and that is what lyrics are. Lyrics are the words to a song. They are written in a specific way for specific reasons. One word is not the same as another, and not just any word will do.

Chattering Away

By four years old, most people will have learned 5,000 words in their first language. That word count doubles by eight years old. By adulthood, that word count will double again! So there are plenty of choices to find the perfect lyrics.

Lyrics by Lute

The word *lyric* has roots that reach back to ancient Greece. The Greek word *lyra* means *lyre*. A lyre was a type of stringed instrument. Greek poems were sometimes played to the **accompaniment** of the lyre. This is part of the history of musical lyrics we know today.

Lyric Levels

Every piece of writing has a reading level. The level tells you how hard the writing is to read. It is based on the words used. The ways the words are arranged can change the level, too.

Think about this sentence: *Kids like to eat candy.* This is for a first-grade reader. A third-grade reading level would look like this: *Kids like eating candy.* For sixth grade, it would be: *Eating candy is something kids like.* Each says the same thing, but the reading level is not the same.

Practice Makes Perfect

A reading level is not based on intelligence. It is about reading development. Think of it like learning to make a free throw in basketball. You have what it takes to make the basket, but you still need to practice. The same is true for reading. Skills build with practice, not intelligence. (But, of course, it is smart to practice!)

A recent study showed that the reading level for pop lyrics has gone down over time. The **average** level a few years ago was third to fourth grade. The average level now is second to third grade. Look at the graph below.

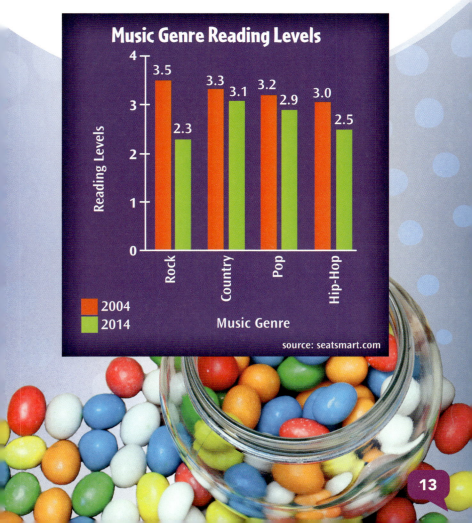

What Makes a Great Lyric?

Songwriters have been searching for the magic key to making hit songs for as long as there have been hit songs. Have they found that key? No way. Every pop song is different, and if there were a key, anyone could easily write a hit. Then what would be the big deal?

What are some reasons that pop songs are **memorable**? Read about the **factors** that many pop songs have in common, especially when it comes to lyrics. Some of the factors also make the songs become hits. Maybe you can use them to write a hit pop song of your own!

Lyrical Dance

Lyrical dance **conveys** moods, such as joy, pain, and love, through movement. The moves are smooth and graceful. Most dancers use songs with lyrics. The words help dancers express themselves.

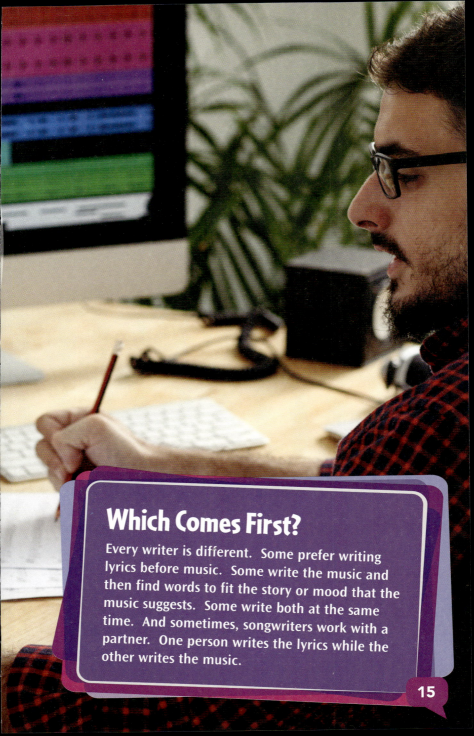

Which Comes First?

Every writer is different. Some prefer writing lyrics before music. Some write the music and then find words to fit the story or mood that the music suggests. Some write both at the same time. And sometimes, songwriters work with a partner. One person writes the lyrics while the other writes the music.

Keep It Simple

Consider these statements: *I love you.* Or, *I deeply admire and am attracted to your many qualities and feel a strong pull in your direction.* Which statement has more **punch**? The first one does, of course. The second one is very **fussy**.

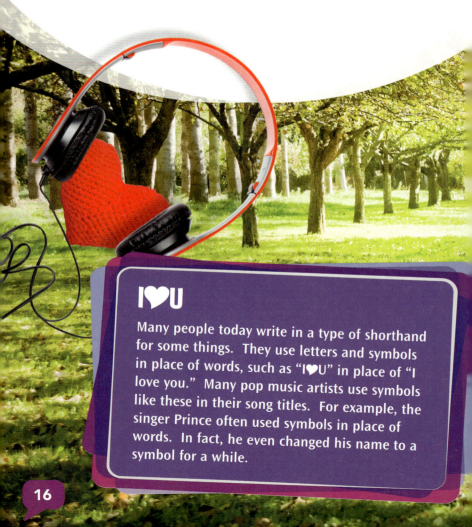

I♥U

Many people today write in a type of shorthand for some things. They use letters and symbols in place of words, such as "I♥U" in place of "I love you." Many pop music artists use symbols like these in their song titles. For example, the singer Prince often used symbols in place of words. In fact, he even changed his name to a symbol for a while.

Great pop lyrics keep it simple. They say what they want to say in a clear way. They also stay "on message" throughout the whole song. If the message of the song is "I love you," the **theme** carries through the whole song. It does not include a part about how the singer also loves petting dogs. And it doesn't talk about the fact that the singer hates mustard on hot dogs. It is all about "I love you."

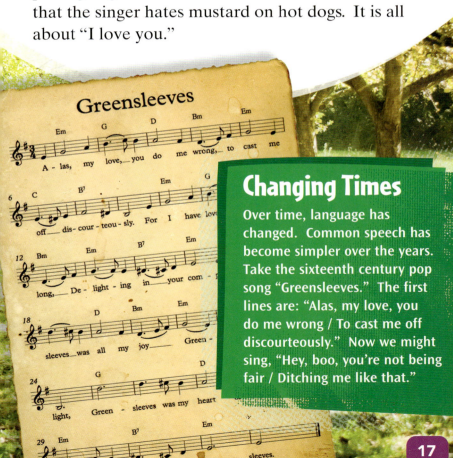

Changing Times

Over time, language has changed. Common speech has become simpler over the years. Take the sixteenth century pop song "Greensleeves." The first lines are: "Alas, my love, you do me wrong / To cast me off discourteously." Now we might sing, "Hey, boo, you're not being fair / Ditching me like that."

How Are You Feeling?

Most people do not want to listen to someone sing about the weather. But they do want to know how the singer *feels*. A song that shares the singer's feelings about the weather might be a big hit. "Stormy Weather" was popular in the 1930s. "I Love a Rainy Night" was a hit in the '80s. Even a song *about* a feeling might make a person feel that way. "Happy" and "Can't Stop the Feeling" have done that in recent years!

As an old song says, "Feelings, whoa-oh-oh, feelings." That's what it is all about in great pop lyrics!

Emoji

The word *emoji* is a mash-up of the Japanese words for *picture* and *character*. Emoji can replace nouns or verbs. They help show feelings or thoughts. Some people like to write songs with emoji where the words should be.

Emoticons

Why write with letters when symbols can say something so well? Emoticons can say a lot with a little. A couple of keys on a keyboard can convey moods. Whether you are :) or :(or :D, emoticons spread the word.

Love, Love, Love

People are very different from one another. But they have some things in common. For example, most people need to love and want to be loved. In fact, love is one of the most frequent themes in pop lyrics. It can be love found, love lost, new love, old love, or the dream of love.

Let's look at some popular songs from the past. In 1975, "Love Will Keep Us Together" was a big hit. "I Will Always Love You" was popular in the 1970s, '80s, and '90s! More recently, "Say Hey (I Love You)" was a hit. The list could go on forever. Clearly, people really love to love a love song!

Love Songs

Songs with *love* in their titles hit their peak in 1980. Then, *love* was in around 14 out of every 100 song titles.

How's That Again?

"I'm blue da ba dee da ba di." Even when the words do not make sense (as in "Blue," a hit from 1999), repeating the words helps to make them memorable. And it helps them stick with listeners. You will find that many pop hits repeat words and phrases.

Words Matter

Now we know that hit pop songs are simple with a clear message. We know they are about a topic most people enjoy. And we know they make people feel something.

But how do writers do all that? They use pop music **techniques**. A common one is rhyme. When song lyrics have catchy rhymes, people remember them and want to sing along. For example, look at some lyrics of "Fight Song" by Rachel Platten: "This is my fight song / Take back my life song / Prove I'm alright song." Words in one line rhyme with words in the next line. Also, the last word of each line repeats, so it rhymes, too. People will be singing this catchy song for years to come!

Short and Sweet

The words of hit pop songs are often short. It is easier to keep a beat and a snappy rhythm with short words and simple rhymes than it is with long words and rhymes. For example, find a rhyme for *smart*. Now, find one for *intelligent*. Which was easier? (Hey, you're pretty smart!)

Hook 'Em

A hook is a line that grabs the listener from the start. It might be a statement, a question, or a story. In hit pop songs, the chorus (the lines of verse that are repeated a lot) can be used as the hook. In "Let It Be" by the Beatles, the phrase "let it be" is repeated 36 times!

Every day, we want to start

And we hope we do our part

ogether we make the world go

r we make a happy soun

Changing Meaning

One little word or phrase can completely change the meaning of a song. What if "I love you" were changed to "I like you"? Or if "I'm sorry" became "whoops"? Writers choose each word to say exactly what they want.

Music can do the same thing. Imagine shifting a beat in a song to change the **emphasis** in a lyric. A changed emphasis can change the meaning, too. For example, what if a beat that hits the word *good* in "He was a good man" hits the word *was* instead? Read it both ways: "He was a *good* man." "He *was* a good man." The meaning changes. It's like a different lyric.

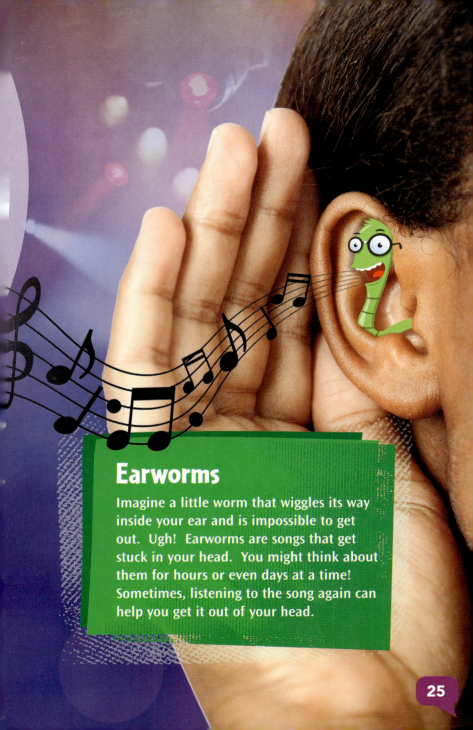

Earworms

Imagine a little worm that wiggles its way inside your ear and is impossible to get out. Ugh! Earworms are songs that get stuck in your head. You might think about them for hours or even days at a time! Sometimes, listening to the song again can help you get it out of your head.

That Would Make a Great Song!

Some studies suggest that humans can think up to 70,000 thoughts a day. That is as many as 75 thoughts each minute. That is more than a thought every second! And any one of those thoughts might be the start of the next great pop song.

Give it a try! Chances are that if you find something interesting, other people will, too. Try turning your thoughts into lyrics. Keep them simple, and make your message clear. Write about something people enjoy. And make people feel something.

Look out, music world—here you come! Now that is something to sing about.

Tech Tunes

You do not have to be human to write a song. Computers can now sort through existing songs and come up with a melody of their own. But the computer still needs help to write the lyrics. One day even that may change.

Glossary

accompaniment—music played to support a singer

average—a level that is typical of a group or class

conveys—communicates

emphasis—added force or special attention

factors—items that help produce a result

fleeting—not lasting long

fussy—too complicated

generation—a group of people born around the same time

genre—a type of music or other art form

medieval—relating to the Middle Ages, which took place from about AD 500 to 1500

memorable—easy to remember

minstrels—musicians and singers from medieval times

number—a song

punch—excitement or interest

slang—words that are part of informal language

techniques—methods for doing something

theme—the main idea or subject

Index

"Can't Stop the Feeling," 18

"Chattanooga Choo Choo," 4

earworms, 25

emoji, 19

emoticons, 19

"Fight Song," 22

"Greensleeves," 17

"Happy," 18

hook, 23

"I Love a Rainy Night," 18

"I Will Always Love You," 20

"Kung Fu Fighting," 4

"Let It Be," 23

"Love Will Keep Us Together," 20

lyre, 11

lyrical dance, 14

medieval, 5

popularity, 7

Prince, 16

reading level, 12

rhyme, 22

slang, 6

"Say Hey (I Love You)," 20

"Stormy Weather," 18

"Sumer Is Icumen In," 5

"Uptown Funk," 4

"Yes! We Have No Bananas," 4, 8

Check It Out!

Books

Didriksen, Erik. 2015. *Pop Sonnets: Shakespearian Spins on Your Favorite Songs.* Quirk Books.

Lukas, Lisa Donovan. 2014. *The Young Musician's Guide to Songwriting: How to Create Music & Lyrics.* Must Write Music.

Tieger, Danny. 2015. *I Am Your Songwriting Journal—Turn Your Amazing Ideas into Awesome Songs!* Peter Pauper Press, Inc.

Websites

Billboard. www.billboard.com/.

"How to Write Songs." *Kidzworld.* www.kidzworld.com.

Stroet, Will. 2015. "A Step-by-Step Guide to Writing Songs with Your Kids." *CBC/Radio-Canada.* www.cbc.ca/parents/play/view/a-step-by-step-guide-to-writing-songs-with-your-kids.

Traynor, Sean. 2010. "Writer's Tips: How to Write Song Lyrics." *Amazing Kids! Magazine.* mag.amazing-kids.org/ak_columns/writers-tips/writers-tips-how-to-write-song-lyrics/.

Try It!

You are going to become the next great hit maker! A big record company wants you to write a song.

❶ Choose one feeling. Think about how to describe it.

❷ Make a list of words and phrases that describe the feeling.

❸ Choose whether to use rhyme. If you use it, where and how will you use it?

❹ Write your lyrics! Remember to keep it simple. Make sure your lyrics make people feel something.

❺ Take on an extra challenge. Create a melody for your song, or choose music you know.

About the Author

Dona Herweck Rice just may be the world's biggest word fan! She loves everything about words—how they look, sound, taste, and feel. She loves to say them, sing them, think them, and be them (although that can get complicated). Dona's superhero identity is Wordy Girl, and she uses her power for good, not evil. She knows there's no greater power in the world than word power—and it's a power everyone can share. Wordy people, unite!